Memory Lane
Leicester

Leicester Mercury
Memory Lane Leicester

Peter Hollins & Steve England

The Breedon Books
Publishing Company
Derby

First published in Great Britain by
The Breedon Books Publishing Company Limited
44 Friar Gate, Derby, DE1 1DA.
1997

ISBN 1 85983 088 9

Printed and bound by Butler & Tanner, Frome, Somerset.
Cover printed by Lawrence Allen, Weston-super-Mare, Somerset.
Colour film supplied by RPS of Leicester.

CONTENTS

FOREWORD

by Councillor Ray Flint
Lord Mayor of Leicester.

BEING born and bred in the City of Leicester, I am very interested in all aspects of the history of Leicester life, in particular the growth of transport through the familiar roads and streets of this great city.

As a boy living in Crown Hills, I remember the old tram terminus on Coleman Road, the shelter of which was constructed from the shell of an old bus! I also recall being quite frightened of outside staircases on the buses when I was taken to visit my aunt in Evington.

Railways, too, are a great passion of mine, I enjoy the history of railways both locally and nationally, and remember clearly that, when I was a young man, Leicester proudly boasted no less than four stations — London Road, Great Central, Belgrave Road and West Bridge.

Nowadays, I enjoy cycling with my wife, Betty, exploring the highways and byways of Leicestershire We are sure readers, too, will find that this 'Memory Lane' book is a reminder of many aspects of our changing and developing city.We hope you will enjoy these photographs which explore, and encapsulate, Leicester's past.

Ray Flint

INTRODUCTION

LEICESTER is a fast-changing city in a fast-changing world. There is hardly a street which has not been touched by change in some way. The only memories of the way it used to be are held in the minds of its citizens and in the photographs from days gone by. In 1995 the *Leicester Mercury* pro-duced *Images of Leicester* – a collection of photo-graphs from our arch-ives which captured something of the way things used to be, dec-ade by decade. This second volume captures images of Leicester and its residents at work and at play, at worship and at war. I am grateful to Steve England and Peter Hollins for their hard work – they have pro-duced something that will help understanding for those too young to remember and stir emotions in those who do.

Nick Carter
Editor
Leicester Mercury

CITYSCAPES

Victoria Park Road corner in 1877 showing the Toll Gate and Toll House which were built in 1851. This is now the site of the London Road/Victoria Park Road/Mayfield Road roundabout.

Northampton Square pictured early this century. The area looks very different today.

The Municipal Buildings pictured before World War One.

Leicester Town Hall and Municipal Buildings seen early this century.

Leicester all dressed up on the occasion of the visit of the Prince of Wales (later King Edward VII) to open the Abbey Park in 1882.

The Newarke and Magazine Gateway as it was when the area lead to the Leicester Castle yard and Trinity Hospital.

Leicester Prison in the early part of the century. Note the tram lines and overhead wires.

A turn-of-the-century view looking down Granby Street with The General News Room in Belvoir Street and the Wellington Hotel on Rutland Street.

The General News Room at the corner of Belvoir Street where until the turn of the century, the news of the day could be read from the London newspapers.

Granby Street and Belvoir Street junction in 1910, when an open-top and an enclosed tram are the only vehicles on show. Most transport up to this period was horse-drawn.

Granby Street in 1908. A Clarendon Park Road tram passes the General Post Office which was built in 1887 on the site of an earlier Post Office, of Georgian style, erected in 1867 and pulled down in 1885. The Bishop Street Post Office opened on 23 July 1935.

A 1906 view of Hinckley Road with an open-topped tramcar making its way up hill. Everyone seems to be dressed in their Sunday best.

London Road and an open-topped tram makes its way from Clarendon Park Road to the city centre in about 1905.

Narborough Road in 1912, opposite Haddenham Road.

The Post Office and Craddock Arms in Knighton, on Chapel Lane, in the 1920s. The pub still stands having changed little and there is still a shop on the corner of Newmarket Street today.

The Guildhall seen here in the late 1950s.

The Pavilion on Abbey Park, Leicester, in 1907, now sadly gone.

St Peter's Road, Leicester, about 1900.

The Coronation Buildings under construction in High Street. They were designed by Arthur Wakerley.

London Road at the turn of the century with a horse tram wending its way towards the town centre.

Horse tram in Applegate Street during the last century.

London Road in about 1905 with the LMS station pictured
on the right.

A tram on a quiet Uppingham Road in 1949.

Bowling Green Street with the rear of the Municipal Buildings and Bishop Street just visible in the background in the late 1930s.

A busy Humberstone Gate, Leicester, in the early 1930s.

Trams in Humberstone Gate in the late 1940s.

A pre-war scene in Humberstone Gate. Lewis's store is on the right. Note the underground toilets in the centre of the road.

Humberstone Gate in the late 1940s. At this time trams were fast disappearing from the city streets, the last one running in 1949.

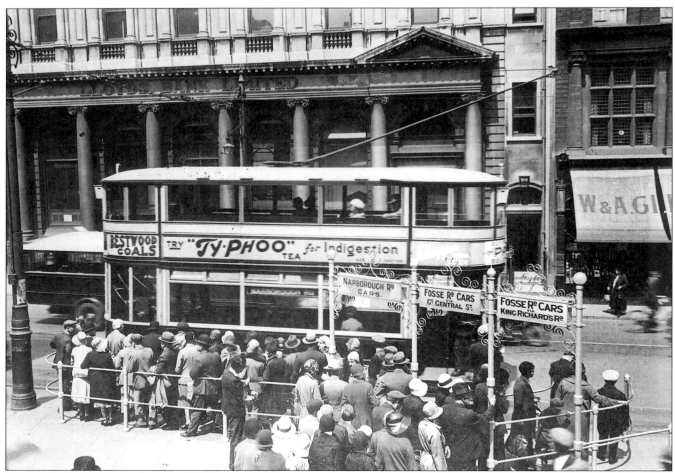

A splendid view of High Street in the 1920s as passengers wait to board a Narborough Road tram. Note the ornate destinations boards.

Charles Street with the junction at Halford Street in the early 1930s. Where the cars are parked later became the Municipal Offices and to the right is now the Alliance & Leicester Building Society offices.

Humberstone Gate pictured in January 1935.

Rutland Street in the 1930s with Charles Street in the background and Granby Street at the forefront.

Charles Street in the 1930s. The buildings in the background made way for the Municipal Offices as Charles Street was modernised.

London Road/Evington Road junction on 19 October 1954. The building on the left is now a bank, but the view has altered little in all these years.

A 1915 view of the Clock Tower.

A quiet Sunday at the Clock Tower in the 1920s.

The Clock Tower in November 1950, a year after the last trams ran.

The junction of Humberstone Road and Wharf Street in the early 1950s. The photograph was taken from the ruins of the Freeman Hardy & Willis building which was bombed during World War Two. The Three Cranes Hotel dominates the picture.

A bird's-eye view of the Clock Tower just after World War Two.

The Clock Tower, seen here in the late 1940s.

The Clock Tower about 1905. The open-topped trams had begun service in 1904, replacing the horse-drawn trams.

Welford Place with a view from Belvoir Street looking down Newarke Street in January 1949. Welford Road is to the left with Pocklington's Walk to the right.

A very busy scene at the Clock Tower in the 1930s.

The Clock Tower *c.*1936. The tramcar on its way to East Park Road via London Road is showing the unusual advertisement for Scott's Solarium Baths. Note the number of cyclists in this scene. During the year ended 31 March 1937, Leicester City Transport received income of £3,546 from advertising on tram cars.

Horsefair Street in March 1955. The Town Hall is in the background.

A busy rush hour around the Clock Tower in the 1930s.

A pre-war view of the Clock Tower in a lunchtime rush hour.

Looking up New Walk on a winter's day in the early 1950s. To the right is now the City Council Building on Belvoir Street.

Leicester Town Hall Square in April 1951.

A bird's eye view looking down on Horsefair Street in August 1952. Simpkin & James is on the left and F.W. Woolworth is in the middle.

A pre-World War Two view from the Clock Tower looking up Gallowtree Gate and Granby Street with Halford Street and Horsefair Street to Millstone Lane crossing it at the top.

Granby Street in July 1938. Kunzle's Cafe is on the right, along with Salts, Raiments. Saxone Shoes is on the left.

Pre-war Granby Street.

Gallowtree Gate in December 1956.

Granby Street probably pictured just after World War Two. Dolcis, Freeman Hardy & Willis and Pochins are some of the shops on the right. The tram is heading for East Park Road.

This pre-war photograph shows Bishop Street in about 1937. The lorry is a Bedford three-tonner belonging to the coal merchant's W. Hercocks.

Digging up the road on Newarke Street in August 1955. The noise must have been deafening from these workmen's drills There were no ear mufflers in those days.

Lee Street Circle car park with Mr Jim Russell, the attendant whose new job at the time was keeping cars *out*. A multi-storey car park was later built on this site.

Granby Street and Horsefair Street junction in February 1958.

Gallowtree Gate in June 1958, looking towards the Clock Tower in the background.

Gallowtree Gate on Boxing Day 1965.

A bird's eye view of High Street in August 1950. New railings had just been erected for queues at the bus stop.

Gallowtree Gate in November 1960.

Gallowtree Gate in December 1956.

Halford Street in November 1960.

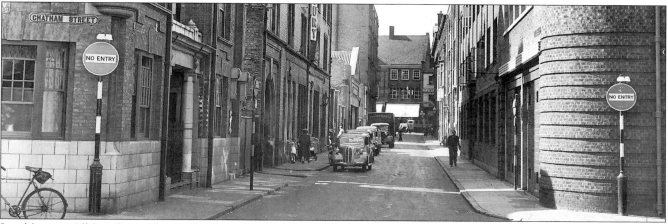

Looking up Albion Street from Chatham Street. The Black Boy Inn is on the left.

A litter strewn corner on Mostyn Street, off Hinckley Road, in October 1956.

Burton's the tailor's on the corner of Eastgates and Churchgate in February 1955.

Braunstone Gate with the Great Central Railway bridge spanning the road, seen here in September 1949. In 1997 it has been decided to demolish the bridge, thus denuding the city of another landmark.

Vulcan Road from Humberstone Road in August 1958.

Biddulph Street, April 1962. There were still plenty of parking spaces on this quiet spring morning.

Knighton Fields Road Bridge viewed from the Welford Road side on August 1958. The Manchester Hotel is on the left.

Langham Bridge on the Leicester-Coventry road at Narborough in September 1952.

Gipsy Lane Bridge in May 1955 with a single-decker bus about to pass beneath it.

Southgate Street in October 1956. The advertisements will evoke nostalgic thoughts for readers of a certain age.

Northampton Square with the Police Station on the left in January 1959.

Churchgate just after 10.15am on a March day in 1962.

The Newarkes in the early 1950s with Leicester College of Art and Technology in the background. A Midland Red double-decker bus waits for passengers to travel to Whetstone via Blaby.

One way traffic in August 1954 as the other side of the road was being repaired.

Newarke Street closed to traffic while road reconstruction takes place in September 1955.

London Road looking towards the town centre on a sunny day in the 1950s.

Belvoir Street on 18 May 1964. The small boy in the foreground will be in early middle-age by now.

In July 1950 this half-mile traffic jam was caused by roadworks to traffic islands and faulty traffic lights. It stretched from Victoria Park to the city centre.

Humberstone Gate in August 1955. With relatively light traffic, that lady can cross the road with her little girl in comfort.

The City Municipal Buildings on Charles Street in 1960.

High Street and Highcross Street in August 1955 with the Commercial Union Buildings on the corner.

Highcross Street off High Street, pictured in January 1961.

The old Free Grammar School on Highcross Street and Freeschool Lane in June 1952.

Highcross Street in the mid-1950s. Next to the Red Lion is an archway, over which is advertised 'Ernest Hornbuckle Ltd, Leather Factors & Importers'.

High Street, November 1958 with Swears & Wells on the left and Lloyds' Bank on the right.

High Street on 28 March 1961 showing huge 'Easter eggs' and baskets of flowers above the road.

High Street, Leicester, on the afternoon of Wednesday, 21 October, 1953.

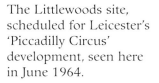

The Littlewoods site, scheduled for Leicester's 'Piccadilly Circus' development, seen here in June 1964.

Horsefair Street and Market Street corner in October 1955. These buildings were demolished to make way for new offices and shops.

This corner property was auctioned in April 1951. It contained Olorenshaw's Restaurant and adjoining premises at the corner of Fox Lane and Humberstone Gate.

Charles Street in September 1955. Most of these buildings are now new offices.

Humberstone Gate on 21 April 1970 with the Bell Hotel standing derelict alongside W.A. Lea & Sons. The ornamental flower troughs in the middle of the road, nicknamed Beckett's Buckets after Mr John Beckett, a former Leicester City Engineer who designed them, were being dismantled at this time.

Charles Street on a sunny day, 14 October 1965. The skyline has changed little in over 30 years.

The traffic island at the junction of Belgrave Gate and Charles Street in September 1963. This view was taken from Epic House.

Looking down Frog Island from Northgate in May 1959.

Uppingham Road in January 1959. Note the Kirby & West milk float.

Hinckley Road in February 1961.

It was a little on the quiet side when this photograph, below, of one of Leicester's traffic headaches – the junction of Evington Road with East Park Road, Mere Road, Beckingham Road and Dashwood Road – in July 1962. However, one can see the potential for a rush-hour jam and it was obvious why the City Council were considering the installation of traffic lights.

Narborough Road near the junction of King Richards Road in July 1961.

Hinckley Road, Leicester, about 1960.

Melton Road, looking from Checketts Road junction towards the city in October 1964.

April 1959 and a beer lorry loaded high with barrels delivers to the LAOB Club in Humberstone Road at Cobden Corner.

A dumped car causes an eyesore on Belgrave Gate in October 1956.

Evington Road at the junction with East Park Road in the early 1960s.

Checketts Road in May 1961. Widening improvements had just been completed after months of work. Here we see traffic turning on to Loughborough Road.

St Barnabas Branch Library at French Road and St Barnabas Road corner, alongside the Post Office telephone exchange, both built in the 1930s.

St Margaret's Bus Station in April 1967. This scene has changed much since then with a new bus station being built to replace these concrete bus shelters.

Welford Road at the junction with Aylestone Road in August 1966.

The Corn Exchange in Leicester Market Place, seen from above in November 1969.

The conical roof of the Melbourne Hall dominates the skyline in this view across the Evington Valley and Highfields, taken from the top of Evington Lane Hill.

Looking down on King Street from the steeple of Holy Trinity Church in May 1957.

Firefighters on the roof of the New Walk Museum in February 1967. Prompt action saved the ceiling caving in and damage was kept to a minimum.

'Prefabs, first erected in Leicester in 1946 and only supposed to last ten years, were used to ease the acute housing shortage after the war. However, many were still in use in the 1970s. Altogether, 570 were built in three main areas of Hinckley Road, off Aikman Avenue, New Parks Estate and Ambassador Road, Evington, with a few in Hughenden Drive, Aylestone.

OPEN ALL HOURS

Georgian buildings at the corner of East Gates and Church Gate around 1880. A directory of 1878 showed A. Sherrard, cabinet maker and upholsterer, at 10 East Gates and Church Gate. A trade advertisement for Alfred Sherrard announced: 'Sole agent for the portable Turkish bath.'

Jackson's the Hatters at 28 Gallowtree Gate, Leicester, pictured about 1913.

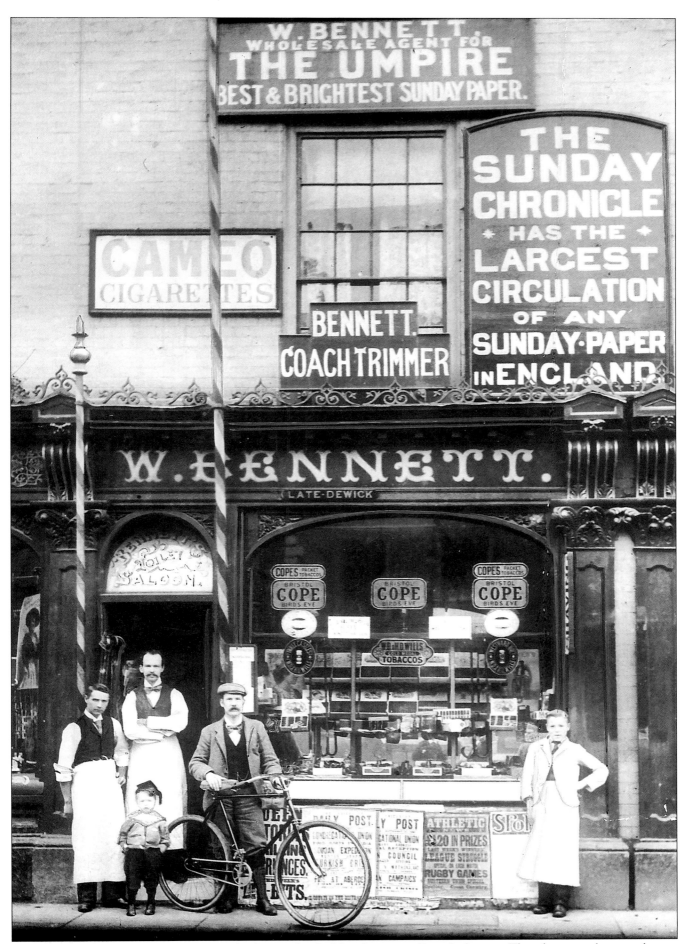

W. Bennett, hairdresser, newsagent and tobacconist, in Humberstone Gate, Leicester. The photograph was taken in 1896.

Children outside a dairy shop in Biddulph Street in the early years of the century. The little boy in the straw hat was killed while serving in France during World War One.

Bonas' Boot Stores of Measham at the turn of the century.

Joints and sides of meat hang outside Stafford's in Victoria Parade in the 1920s.

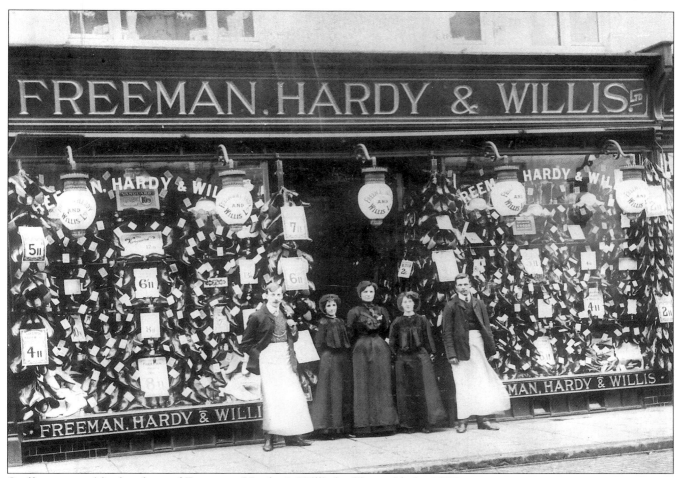

Staff pose outside the shop of Freeman, Hardy & Willis in Cheapside in 1908.

The Post Office at Frog Island, Leicester, pictured about 1904.

348 Harrison Road in Belgrave in 1919, showing Harry Barrow and family.

Archie Brewster and a boy employee pictured outside a shoe repair shop at 208 Loughborough Road in Leicester just after World War One.

W.H. Sercombe, the family butchers on Cavendish Road, seen here about 1920.

W.W. White's ironmongery shop window on Upper Conduit Street, Leicester. Their proud boast was that all their brushes were locally manufactured.

Thomas Whysall, pawnbrokers at 182 Humberstone Road in Leicester. It must have been quiet a task to remove everything from the front of the premises each night.

G.A. Brown, confectioners of Upper Conduit Street, Leicester, pictured before World War One with a fine selection of sweets and chocolates on view. Note the aspidistra in the top window.

The Post Office at North Kilworth was opened in 1847 by Stephen Howkins. This 1902 view shows Stephen's son, James, who took over the business from his father.

Mr John Weston Jesson's butcher's shop, known as J's of Gumley, pictured early this century. It was left untouched for more than 40 years, like a time capsule, and was only recently uncovered and the contents put up for auction.

A travelling butcher pausing on his round at Fleckney in 1910. He tended to the horse and cut up his meat without clean water to hand, and his chopping block was open to dust and insects. What would a modern-day health inspector make of it all?.

The Highfields Dairy, from which the Kirby& West business grew, over 100 years ago.

Remember the days when milk deliveries were made by horse and cart? Mr Walter Newbury pictured outside his mother's shop and dairy in Highfields.

Charles Barwell, the Goadby and Nosely carrier, pictured at the junction of Scraptoft Lane and Uppingham Road at the spot where the Trocadero Cinema was later built, although, alas, that too has now gone.

The Old North End Steam Bakery van outside St Leonard's Vicarage (now demolished) in Woodgate in 1914. The bakery was in Dunton Street.

Delivery boy Tom Mould with Price's Bakery's horse and cart in 1907. Young Tom was killed in 1916, aged 26, at Passchendaele.

Frears' Bakery's first bread delivery van, pictured around 1926.

Rossa's sold cream ices from this converted motorised hearse. Don and Tony Rossa are pictured with a customer.

'Business as usual' for Mr George Needham at his watch and clock shop at 77 Southgates.

According to legend this was the spot where King Richard III slept before the Battle of Bosworth Field. For many years this was the site of the Blue Boar Inn. Mr Walter Pollins, a sewing machine expert, traded here in Highcross Street for over 30 years before closing his shop in 1961 when it was demolished under an improvement scheme.

Ye Olde Village Shoppe and Post Office in Braunstone in 1933.

Leicester people queuing for food in outside the Home & Colonial Stores in 1917. German torpedoes nearly succeeded in starving Britain into surrender.

The Belvoir Street city pram firm of Robothams Ltd, which had served Leicester for 66 years, closed down early in 1973. Known as Baby's Kingdom it boasted that it sold everything that any child could possibly need for the first six years of its life.

The Coffee Stall in Humberstone Gate in May 1963.

The old 'cash by railway' system operated between counter and cashier in the Beehive Shop on Silver Street. Here, Miss H.L. Grimley demonstrates the method of transporting money.

The frontage of the Beehive Shop on Silver Street, pictured here in October 1962.

The nearly-completed Littlewoods Store on the Humberstone Gate-Haymarket site. which was later opened by Sir Barnett Janner MP in May 1967.

Granby Street and Belvoir Street junction in April 1958. Once again it is remarkable to see how little traffic there was about.

Testing the floodlights on the Municipal Offices in April 1953, two months before Queen Elizabeth II was crowned.

The junction of Charles Street and Belgrave Gate in June 1961, showing part of the new traffic island which had just been installed.

The W.A. Lea & Sons store on Humberstone Gate, Leicester, was taken over by Debenhams in 1957.

City centre scene prior to the Haymarket development in the early 1960s. The large gap in the buildings on the right would eventually be filled by Littlewoods.

The walk-through between Marks & Spencer and Lewis's stores on Fox Lane in August 1965.

Granby Street on a wet day in May 1955.

Simpkin & James, one of Leicester's favourite city centre shops who were purveyors of fine foods and wines, sited on Horsefair Street and pictured here in the 1960s.

Kunzles Café on Granby Street (left) and Moreton's Café (right) both pictured in the 1950s.

This scene inside a pre-war Leicester provision store in Hotel Street revives memories of the days when a pound note would fill a big basket of groceries, when a penny would provide a long ride on a tramcar, 2d would buy a paper packet of five cigarettes, a shilling would pay for a round of drinks, 10s would fill a tank of petrol, and £100 would cover the cost of a new car.

In 1936, the furniture shops were offering oak bedsteads – 'superb value' – for 79s 6d and 'luxurious lounge suites' for 11 guineas. Wine merchants were selling 'genuine' port and sherry' for 3s 9d a bottle, or £1 a dozen, milliners had hats for business girls at 3s 11d and 4s 11d, and the LNER were offering Sunday rail trips to London for 5s 6d in a buffet car train, departure 10.35am.

Radio sets were on offer for 1s 6d a week and the used car advertisements were offering a '1931 Morris Cowley Saloon at £22 10s.'

In the accommodation world there were such offers as 'Humberstone Road, large well furnished room, electric lighted, private stove, bathroom, modern grate, no children. 12s a week'. New houses were on offer at £450, £499 and £600. Of course, wages were a fraction of what they are today.

The Dover Café on Granby Street. It made way for a modern store in 1957. Previously it had housed the Capital T Club.

The old fish and chip shop at the bottom of Dover Street in August 1960.

Charnwood Street, Leicester, in November 1961. It must have been after school, or maybe it was a Saturday.

What delights there were to be had in Paddy's Swag Shop on Charnwood Street in Leicester, pictured here in the 1950s.

Evington Road in August 1955. In the space of a lifetime the area had changed from a quiet country lane to what was then described as 'one of the most completely appointed shopping centres in the whole of Leicester's suburbia'.

The corner of Evington Road and Mere Road in November 1963.

Two views of Evington Road in December 1961. The newsagent's business at the corner of Sawley Street was Prince & Williams. Gaunt's hairdressers was on the corner of Lyme Road.

A row of new shops opened on the Greengate Lane Estate, Birstall, early in 1960.

The Fish Market, designed by local architect William Millcan who was active at the turn of the century, seen here in August 1977.

The entrance to the Corridor Arcade in the Market Place in July 1961. Ten shops and the offices above, known as Corridor Chambers, were about to be auctioned.

The Fruit Market on Halford Street in September 1951.

Lewis's store (above, left) was one of the city's most famous landmarks. It was opened on Saturday, 21 March 1936 and comprised 77 departments on four floors with a restaurant on the top floor. Alas it is now gone. In 1968, Knossington Post Office (above, right) claimed the distinction of being the smallest in the Midlands. Here, Postmistress Mrs Mary Greswell cleans the windows of the 10ft by 6ft hut.

The village Post Office at Packington pictured in March 1959. This was also a humble office, but it served the local population admirably.

EARNING A
LIVING

Wheelwright Samuel Harrison pictured in Hinckley Road, Leicester Forest East, about 1920.

Three generations of Gearys have run a carpentry business in Billesdon. Taken around 1910, this picture shows second generation owner Mr John Geary on the left.

Five figures who were engaged in the local cigar business in its heyday. It was something of a local industry in the latter part of last century and employed many girls in the skilled craft of making cigars entirely by hand. These gentlemen pose before Free Trade posters in 1906. One notice reads: 'Treat Foreigners as They Treat Us. Treat Kinsmen Better Than You Treat Foreigners.'

Above left: The home of Tom Hoskins at 133 Beaumanor Road, Leicester, in May 1972. Hoskins was one of the few family breweries still functioning in Britain at that time, although today, of course, there are many independent brewers once more. Above, right: This 1909 picture shows members of the Anchor Tenants Building Department, whose motto was 'Not Greater Wealth but Simpler Pleasures'. General manager and architect Mr George Hern stands on the left.

Left: These Lutterworth tradesmen gathered for this photograph before the turn of the last century. Represented are a plumber, blacksmith, brewer, draper, grocer, bootmaker, chemist and the police.

Griswold knitters outside the Lutterworth Baptist Church in 1890. 'Griswold' was a knitting technique.

Blacksmith's house and part of the workshop in Medbourne, pictured around 1899. In the trap is Mr Eli Barlow and his son Bert. His youngest son, Len, is at the horse's head. Mr Barlow had other branches at Great Easton, Ashley, Blaston and Nevill Holt Hall, which was the home of shipping magnate Sir Bache Cunard.

The Leicester Corporation Mill Lane refuse destructor with the conveyor belt taking rubbish to the furnaces. Note the dustbin lorry disgorging its load into the pit where men are sorting it for disposal.

Leicester Corporation Destructor in West Humberstone in November 1938. Slabs are being made from crushed refuse and a mixture of cement.

A busy scene in Leicester, showing the hosiery shopfloor at A.H. Broughton's in 1928.

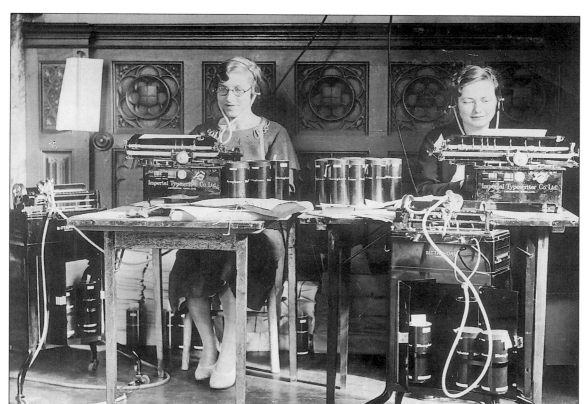

The first ever use of the Dictaphone machine at the 1934 League of Industry Conference which was presided over by Lord Nuffield. Speech recordings were transcribed in the conference office.

Employees of N. Corah & Sons, St Margaret's Works, gather for a photograph in 1919. The firm's factory and warehouses covered nearly six acres and employed 2,500 people.

Mr John Brindley, managing director of Couture Marketing Ltd, seen in the company's Burbage factory with model Annette-Patricia in November 1979.

Drum assembly line at the Premier Drum Co Ltd, South Wigston, in February 1966.

The Furnace, a relic of Moira's industrial history, which ceased production in the middle of the last century. The tree growing on the top of the building had been there since around 1910, but by 1966 seemed to have drawn all the sustenance it could get out of the brickwork.

Photographed during their visit to the Premier Drum factory at South Wigston in 1978 are four aspiring young drummers. From left to right they are Ethan Johns (son of top British record producer Glyn Johns), Zak and Jason Starkey (the sons of Ringo Starr) and Dylan Jones, son of former Small Faces drummer Kenny Jones (at rear) who replaced the late Keith Moon in The Who in the same year.

The Old Smithy in Main Street, Houghton-on-the-Hill, closed by 1971 because the blacksmith had moved to Billesdon.

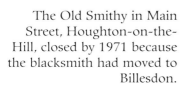

With the addition of a fourth-floor executive suite in 1960, the British United Shoe Machinery Company's premises in Belgrave Road was to get a streamlined new look.

MacDonald Road showing the British United Shoe Machinery Company on the left in February 1962.

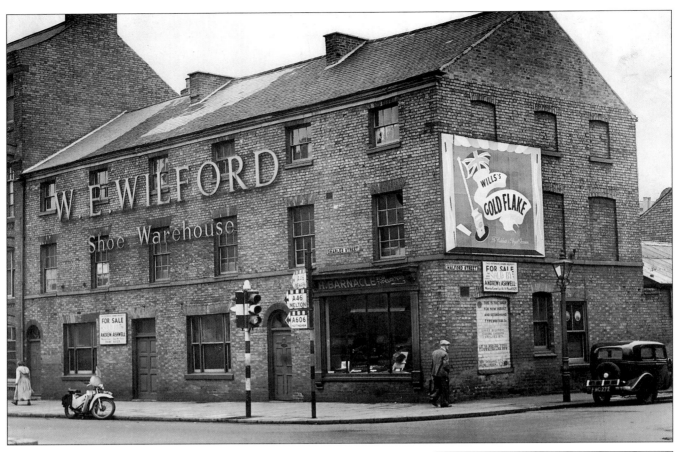

W.E. Wilford's shoe warehouse on the corner of Charles Street and Halford Street, Leicester, in June 1953.

This late Georgian or William IV terrace in Northampton Road, Market Harborough, was a good specimen of early 19th-century homes. It became the offices of W. Symington & Co, the soup firm which was founded in 1827.

Symington's corset factory in Market Harborough, seen from across the square in June 1962. At one time it had been a carpet factory.

Workers seen leaving one of Anstey's two footwear factories at lunchtime in February 1960.

Monument to a courageous venture, the Sperope factory in Kirkby Road, Barwell, a co-partnership concern which Will Harvey and other workers founded in the early 1890s. The name is a partnership of Latin and English (*spero* = to look for, to expect, to hope).

Above: A.B. Taylor & Son, boot manufacturers of 100 Havelock Street, Leicester, closed in January 1958. Next door is the Regal Cinema which closed in May, the following year.

Above: Snibston Colliery on Ashby Road in Coalville, pictured in June 1962. Opened in 1832, in 1986 it became the Snibston Discovery Park, a major tourist attraction.

The old brickworks at Broughton Astley being demolished in March 1959.

The North Bridge Engineering Company in Abbey Lane was started by Mr Walter Frisby with a £100 lathe which turned out repetition parts for tanks and aircraft in 1940. In April 1960, the precision engineering company was the subject of a £250,000 takeover by Clifford Motor Components Ltd of Birmingham.

Two thatched white-washed cottages in Church Walk, Hinckley, nearly the last of the dwellings in which the town's hosiery industry had its beginnings, pictured in 1959 just before being demolished.

The Old Stockingers Cottages in Lower Bond Street, Hinckley, in 1961. They were thatched with an attractive sedge ridge in a herring-bone pattern.

A picture to commemorate the visit to Lutterworth in 1988 of the inventor of the jet engine, the late Sir Frank Whittle, 50 years after the test run of the world's first jet engine at Ladywood Works, hangs in a place of honour in the Town Hall. Mr Nigel Webster is seen presenting the picture to Town Hall trustees in 1990.

TIME GENTLEMEN, PLEASE!

The Admiral Nelson in Humberstone Gate. Its history goes back to the early 18th century, when it was a cottage with outbuildings, barns, stabling, orchards and gardens.

The Blue Lion Hotel, now the site of the Jarvis Grand Hotel in Leicester.

The Red Lion public house in Sanvey Gate with Mr Thomas Colinson standing in the doorway, with his wife Sarah in the white apron.

The Cricketers Rest Inn, Abbey Gate. On the lamp above the door proclaims 'Pleasure boats for hire.'

The Saracen's Head at the turn of the century. It boasts an inn on the site for some 700 years. The name is connected with a coat of arms borne by the victors in the Crusades. It was also the centre in Leicester for Naval recruitment.

The Lion and Lamb Hotel next to the Pelican Inn in Gallowtree Gate, pictured in 1876. The Pelican was the last pub in Gallowtree Gate and was sold in 1968. The Lion and the Lamb Hotel site was later occupied by Central Buildings, where Kemp's Clock is situated.

Regulars at the Dolphin Inn on Lichfield Street pose for the camera around the turn of the century. The dog's name was Rose.

More regulars, this time outside the Charles Napier on the corner of Causeway Lane and White Street, pictured around 1913.

Stewards at the Humberstone Gate branch of Manchester Oddfellows in 1914.

The Royal Standard Inn at 21 Charles Street, Leicester. Alfred Allen was the publican there in 1922.

The Antelope at 16 Silver Street in Leicester. This was a popular venue for sportsmen with facilities for pool, billiards and boxing.

The King William at Mountsorrel about the turn of the century. John Green was the licensee and so presumably this is him with his wife, son and the family pet.

An early photograph of the George and Dragon at Primethorpe. As was the custom, this looks as if it was once just an ordinary dwelling house that became a drinking establishment.

The Old Plough Inn Birstall in 1921. The little girl on the steps was three years old then. As Mrs A. Ward, with six children and 11 grandchildren, she later recalled, "These were happy days."

Left: The Blue Ball Inn in Braunstone, near Oakham, in 1903.

Below, left: The Greyhound Hotel in the Beast Market in Lutterworth pictured in the 1930s. Sadly it is no more.

Below, right: The Grand Hotel on the corner of Granby Street and Belvoir Street in August 1957. What a magnificent building it is.

The 170-year-old Wellington Hotel on the corner of Granby Street and Rutland Street in June 1957.

The Bell Hotel next to W.A. Lea & Sons on the corner of Humberstone Gate and Charles Street, photographed in 1963.

The Stag and Pheasant Hotel and Restaurant on Humberstone Gate in October 1958. This building was opened in 1905.

The Tower Pub in Humberstone Gate, pictured in 1960.

The White Hart Hotel in Haymarket, pictured in October 1958 before redevelopment.

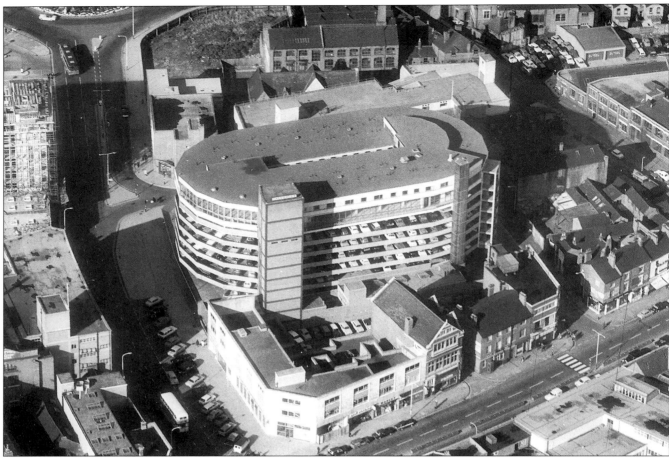

Abbey Motor Hotel, now the Hotel St James, Abbey Street, seen in November 1966. It was opened in April the following year.

The beginning of the end for the Hotel Victory, Great Central Street, Leicester, in Augus 1967.

The Swan with Two Necks at 58 Granby Street, Leicester, in March 1959. The name is said to have derived from the custom of marking, or 'nicking', swans' bills to signal ownership. There are, however, at least two prominent English families whose crests bear a swan with two necks and even the Habsburgs used the device at one time.

A drink ban was imposed in Harrison Road in 1958. But that did not bother the locals at the Victoria Jubilee. It faced both Harrison Road and Leire Street, and its Leire Street address meant customers could carry on drinking!

Newfoundpool Working Men's Club on Beatrice Road in March 1958.

The Whimsey Inn at Ibstock in January 1951.

The Ram Hotel at Ibstock in January 1951, considered to be the oldest in the pub village.

The New Inn at Enderby on a warm summer's day in the 1950s.

The Peacock Hotel in The Square, Market Harborough, in June 1962. It was then about 200 years old and legend had it that the Peacock stood on the site of an earlier inn, the Mermaid.

Thise picturesque view of the Rose and Crown Inn at Thurnby was photographed in September 1951.

Left: The Queen's Head Inn on High Street, Barwell, pictured in January 1959.

The Red Cow Inn on Hinckley Road, Leicester Forest East, on 20 October 1960.

The George Inn in Hinckley, pictured in August 1958. Note the two delivery lorries, one from Schweppes, the other from the local firm of Jones Beverages.

The Cock Inn in Peatling Magna in May 1958. Beyond the inn is pictured Brookhill Farm.

Legend has it that the original boundaries of Leicestershire, Stafford-shire, Derbyshire and Warwickshire once met under the headstone of the Four Counties Inn at No Man's Heath, near Measham.

The official opening of the Quorn Country Hotel in January 1984. Among the guests were Rhani, a 14-year-old Indian elephant, with Leicester model Gaynor Simpson getting a lift.

RURAL RETREATS

This view shows the main street in Woodhouse Eaves. The postcard from which it is taken was posted at 5.45pm on 20 August 1918, shortly before World War One ended, and shows mainly children and women as most men were away fighting in the trenches.

The windmill at Woodhouse Eaves in 1918. This card was also postmarked August 1918 and the message read: 'Dear Dad, I am alright and just going into the woods. Hope to see you on Wednesday. Love from Edie.' It was sent to Mr E.Turner at 120 Hartopp Road, Clarendon Park, Leicester.

A lovely glimpse back in time to 1910 and Thorpe End in Melton Mowbray. On the left is Moore's bakers and confectioners and on the right The Whitehouse public house.

Nottingham Street, Melton Mowbray, early this century.

Market Street, Ashby-de-la-Zouch, about 1900.

Loughborough Town Hall in the latter part of the last century.

Belvoir Castle near Melton Mowbray, another view from an old postcard.

Whatton House between Kegworth and Loughborough, in the north of the county.

The River Swift and Bridge at Lutterworth at the turn of the century.

The magnificent viaduct stretching away near East Norton earlier this century.

Loughborough High Street at the turn of the century, showing the Bull's Head Hotel.

Market day in Market Harborough in the 1930s. There seems to be a traffic jam building up.

How did we get into this mess? A Midland Red bus and a van locked together in the narrow part of Moat Street, Wigston Magna in July 1962.

The Common at the junction of Evington Lane (once picturesquely marked Puck Lane and The Common) in May 1962.

Oadby in July 1962. The Co-op van has just arrived and a lady pushes her pram along a sunlit street.

Oadby in July 1960. The village main street with its cottages, pubs and parish church.

Billesdon Market Cross in March 1960. The conductor is about to board his Midland Red double-decker parked near the Post Office for the trip back to Leicester. One of the posters on the right is advertising a film being shown at the ABC Cinema in Leicester entitled *A Summer Place* starring Richard Egan, Dorothy Maguire, Sandra Dee, Arthur Kennedy and Troy Donohue.

More traffic congestion, this time in Castle Street, Hinckley (the A47), in October 1960.

Belvoir Road, Coalville, in the 1960s. Newspaper delivery boys waiting for the *Leicester Mercury* van to arrive.

Brook Street, Barkby, in July 1964, with the appropriately-named Brookside Inn.

The Railway Inn, Ketton, in August 1963 with St Mary's Church in the background.

A stonemason at work on the Ashby Loudoun Memorial with the help of a Burton Upon Trent Fire Brigade turntable ladder in March 1957.

Uppingham Market Place with the Falcon Hotel in May 1961.

The Primethorpe end of Broughton Astley. The George and Dragon Inn, Mr Frank Hall's garage and the old Liberal Hall, used by the Primethorpe Hosiery Company, all pictured on 14 March 1959.

Vehicles parked outside the Midland Bank at Market Bosworth in March 1960.

In the rush of motorways, by-passes, and clearways, one tends to forget that such things as fords still exist. This is Marston Trussell in August 1965 with an Austin 1100 exiting from the ford.

Market Harborough in February 1968. The Three Swans Hotel is on the left.

Thatched roofs at Narborough village in October 1962. The road to the left is to the railway station, Littlethorpe, Cosby and Whetstone.

The George Hotel in High Street, Melton, in 1912. It appears to be market day as an array of carts and traps crowd the thoroughfare. No doubt the owners are partaking of a jar or two inside the George Hotel.

A 1911 view of Hallaton and a parade complete with marching band prepares to set off past the Old Royal Oak Inn.

ON THE MOVE

The decorative frieze above Leicester's Clock Tower pavement where Thomas Cook set up his business in the second half of the last century.

Thomas Cook (1808-1892). Modern travel roots go back to 1841 when Cook hired a train to take a party from Leicester to Loughborough. The success of this led to him setting up the travel business which still bears his name. Ten years later he transported thousands of people to the Great Exhibition at the Crystal Palace. The Paris Exhibition of 1855 drew Thomas Cook abroad for the first time, followed by trips all over the continent. Cook joined the Prince of Wales at the opening of the Suez Canal in 1869, and by 1880 the firm had a fleet of steamers and had obtained a monopoly on the Nile passenger service. Thomas Cook is buried in Welford Road Cemetery.

The Leicester-Swannington Railway level crossing at Fosse Road North. The line was opened in 1832 and consisted of a single track except at stations and on the Bagworth incline where there were two sets of rails. George and Robert Stephenson were on the footplate of the *Comet* when it first travelled over this level crossing. The crossing was replaced by a bridge in 1899.

Campbell Street
Railway Station
which was
demolished to
make way for the
London Road
Midland Station.

London Road Railway Station
pictured at the turn of the century.

A late 1920s bird's eye view of Leicester's Midland Station on London Road.

Children trainspotting on Swain Street bridge above the London Road Station. Although they look as if they are on the parapet, they are in fact well back on a separate span which cuts off the pavement from the roadway. The engine sheds can be seen on the right, with the main line on the left.

An aerial view showing Leicester London Road Station in November 1969. To the middle left on the waste ground now stands the Post Office building and a block of high-rise flats.

The Belgrave Road Great Northern Railway Station in June 1964, which by this time had closed for good. It was built in 1883.

Heading for the sea, ex-LNER B1 No. 61092 makes a flamboyant start from Leicester Belgrave Road Station with an East Coast excursion on a Saturday morning in May 1958.

Taper Scot Class No. 46158, The Loyal Regiment, storms southward on the 5.15pm Nottingham-Marylebone express on 24 August 1963, near East Leake.

Blaby Railway Station pictured in October 1961.

A beautiful flower-bedecked garden at Glen Parva Railway Station with stationmaster Mr S.F. Willsmer attending to a hanging basket of geraniums. The station was one of the entries for the best-kept railway station garden competition for the Leicester District in August 1951.

Ashby Railway Station in May 1961. The lines of the old Burton & Ashby Light Railway were still visible at the time.

South Wigston Railway Station, derelict in October 1964 with the weeds well established since closure.

The Ratby Railway Goods Depot in September 1954 with the level crossing at New Bridge. The line was closed to passenger traffic in 1929, after which coal was the commodity most handled here. The stretch of line was from Desford Colliery to West Bridge Wharf. The Desford-Glenfield line follows the same route as the original Leicester-Swannington Railway constructed by George Stephenson and his son, Robert, in 1830-1834. It was designed to bring coal direct to Leicester.

The level crossing on the Ellistown-Nailstone Road. With a coal train on the main Leicester-Burton line in February 1952. The line connected Nailstone Colliery with the sidings at Bagworth Station.

Frisby-on-the-Wreake Railway Station near Melton Mowbray, seen here in June 1961 shortly before closure. No. 90208 pulls a short freight train.

Lutterworth Station in August 1957 with a freight train pulled by 92087, a BR 9F 2-10-0.

Shepshed Railway Station in January 1962 with an ex-LMS 4F freight engine and crew. The station master, Mr H. Hardy, stands next to the guard and wheeltapper. Mr Charles Matthews, his wife, Joyce, and daughter, Susan, chat with the railwaymen.

Ex LMS Ivatt class 2MT 2-6-2T taking on water at Leicester London Road Railway Station in the mid-1960s with a young train spotter looking on.

Brush Locomotive Works in Loughborough with diesels under construction.

A coal cart belonging to G. Loomes, coal merchant of Myrtle Road, has just won first prize in a procession or parade in the early 1920s.

Collin's the coach builders in the Beast Market, Lutterworth, pictured in the last century.

A fully loaded coach on Kendall & Sons' work's outing in 1898 to Charnwood Kendall & Sons started in Northampton Street in 1870.

An early 1920s motorcycle and wicker sidecar. The lady looks anything but happy at the prospect of a breezy 30mph spin and is wrapped to combat the weather.

Mr Cumming and family on a 1923 Aero Douglas motorcycle combination.

George K. Debenham on his Panther 600cc double adult motorcycle and sidecar. After World War Two, few people could afford motor cars and so growing families turned to the motorcycle combination.

Batchelor Bowles garage in the 1920s.

The Savoy Service Station at Anstey in April 1961.

The Olympia Service Station on Narborough Road in April 1959 with its futuristic-looking canopy.

Judging by the number plate – BC7 – this car must have been one of the first to be registered in Leicester and the picture shows the Bennett family about to go on a Sunday drive.

A De Dion Boulton in Granby Place, Leicester, early this century with a car full of tobacco merchants who were on a trip to Longcliffe Wood. They are pictured outside Percy Baker's tobacco shop. Mr Baker is the one with a cigar and cap, fifth from the left.

This photograph was taken near Kibworth in the early 1920s when motoring was still the domain of the rich.

The most famous number plate in Leicester must be ABC1, which for years has adorned the Lord Mayor of Leicester's limousine. Here it is seen in 1952.

Erecting concrete posts and barrier rails at the Welford Road traffic island in March 1937. The prison stands in the background.

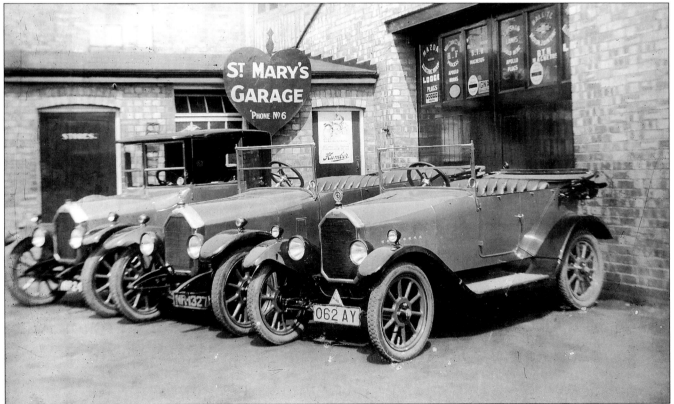

St Mary's Garage in Market Harborough in the 1920s. The motor cars are brand-new Humbers placed on the forecourt for sale.

A steam wagon belonging to Melton Mowbray Rural District Council pictured in 1921 with roadworkers or 'Lengthmen' who were paid half an hour's pay for every mile over two miles they laid. No protective clothing was provided but they received an allowance of a shilling a day when working with a tar boiler as this was considered likely to damage clothing.

Police Constable John ('Dick') Adams of Duncan Road, Aylestone, on point duty at the Clock Tower on 15 June 1936.

Tram tracks being laid on Narborough Road in 1904.

The first of three water cars to be delivered came in 1904 and was numbered 100. Built by Dick Kerr of Preston, the car could hold 2,500 gallons and was equipped for snow ploughing and rail grinding. It is seen here at the Belgrave terminus in 1904.

Car No. 101 of the Leicester City Tramways. This first canopy-top car delivered to the Leicester undertaking came in 1905. It was different to others in the batch, being fitted with a sort of semi vesticle around the upper deck balcony seats. It is seen at the Belgrave terminus when new.

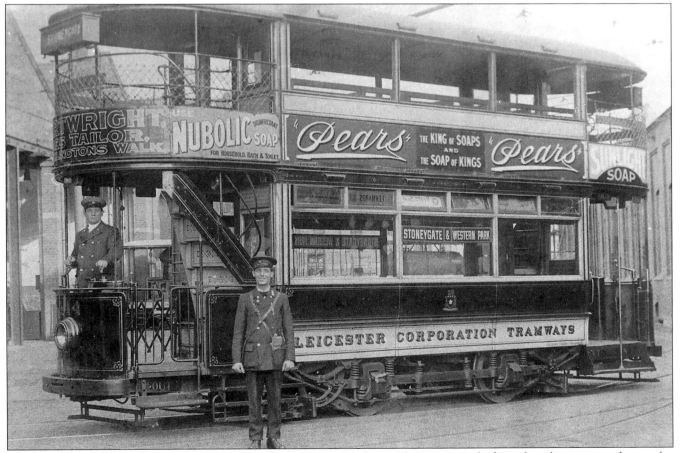

The tramcar served Leicester for many years, beginning with horse-drawn trams before electric trams took over in 1904 and lasting until 1949. This scene shows a tram outside the Abbey Park Depot prior to World War One.

A tram passes the White Hart Hotel, Leicester, in the 1920s. Note everyone is wearing a hat.

With most men away fighting in World War One, women were called upon to run essential services. Here we see a group of women drivers and conductresses supported by a few men.

Motormen, conductors, an inspector and the manager of Leicester City Tramways seen here about 1904.

Tram No. 150 in old livery with the word 'Leicester' removed by wartime censorship orders, and car No. 39 in later livery picking up Jehovah's Witnesses from a convention in September 1941.

Leicester's last tram leaving the Clock Tower on 9 November 1949, on its final journey on a wet wintry day.

A Leicester City double-decker bus specially decked out to mark the Silver Jubilee of the reign of King George V in 1935. This photograph was taken at the corner of Broad Avenue, Green Lane Road and Coleman Road.

September 1939 and trees and kerbs are painted with white stripes to help in the blackout as war looms.

A 1939 AEC Renown six-wheeler No. 324 pictured new in Humberstone Gate. and about to turn into Charles Street.

A bus conductress on a Leicester Corporation double-decker bus during World War Two.

A Leyland Titan double-decker at the junction of Welford Road and Clarendon Park Road in 1937. The row of houses were built in 1890. Belgravia as advertised on the side of the bus was the trade name of M. Snaith & Sons Ltd, who had premises in Belgrave Gate.

An AEC Regent double-decker of Leicester City Transport at Western Park terminus in the late 1930s.

An accident at the junction of Winchester Avenue and Narborough Road in 1947. An Austin saloon car is struck by a double-decker No. 227 en route from Welford Place to Braunstone Estate.

Crowds leaving the Greyhound Stadium on Blackbird Road in the late 1940s.

In November 1952 this is what a gale did to the Leicester Corporation bus garage in Abbey Park Road. A big section of a high brick wall crashed through the roof.

This bus driver forgot he had a double-decker bus and failed to negotiate the Lancaster Road bridge in November 1965. Fortunately only two passengers were aboard and neither was badly hurt. Over many years this bridge has been the scene of similar accidents involving double-decker buses.

Leicester's first-ever motorised fire appliances, purchased by the Corporation from the Wolsey Company in 1903.

A fire appliance outside the Grand Hotel on 29 September 1959.

A Model T Ford police car in the early 1920s, the first to be issued to the Leicester force.

A Morris Isis police car outside Illston Cottage Post Office in the 1950s.

A Jaguar police car pictured in February 1962.

Braunstone Aerodrome pictured on 5 January 1938.

A helicopter belonging to Captain Anthony Everard is inspected by curious schoolchildren at Glenfield Junior School in September 1966. Mrs J. Cunningham explains the salient features to her brood.

The canals were once an important form of transportation. Here a woman bargee ties up her barge at the turn of the century.

England's smallest county brings its guns to bear on the County Rooms, Leicester, where the Commission on Boundaries was hearing views on Rutland's future in July 1960. 'HMS Rutland' is seen here sailing past a group of well wishers. In 1997, of course, the county of Rutland reappeared on the map of England.

CHURCHES AND CHAPELS

St Peter's Church, Leicester, pictured about 1905.

The great fire at St George's in Leicester on 5 October 1911.

Leicester Cathedral's Vaughan Porch was built in 1896-97 as a memorial to Edward Thomas Vaughan, Vicar of St Martin's between 1802 and 1820 and his three sons, who followed in their father's footsteps. Above the entrance is a frieze of seven men, all connected with history of the diocese.

Leicester London Road Congregational Church pictured in July 1960, when it was sold for £21,400 as a site for shopping development.

The demolition of the former 103-year-old Congregational Church on London Road in September 1960. It had closed in December the previous year.

Joseph Hansom may have been inspired by a Melton Mowbray pork pie when he designed the chapel on Belvoir Street in Leicester. In November 1951 the building became the Leicester Adult Education Centre.

The Charles Street, Leicester, Baptist Church was built in 1830 on the site of a Bethesda Chapel, which belonged to a section of the Methodist body called the 'Kilhamites' from the name of their leader. The opening services took place on 19 January 1831.

The chancel at
Leicester Cathedral
photgraphed in
December 1957.

Bagworth Village Church with
its ancient tower, probably
Early English, as it was in
September 1966.

St John the Divine in Buckminster,
photographed in 1970.

Great Stretton was once bigger than the
neighbouring village of Little Stretton, but over
the centuries it dwindled until all that was left
was the tiny church of St Giles. Robert de
Stretton, chaplain to the Black Prince and the
Bishop of Lichfield, was baptised there.

Melton's Baptist Chapel, which was built in 1872.

The weather presents a fairy-tale quality to this view of Kibworth Parish Church in December 1964.

The Parish Church of St Peter, Higham-on-the-Hill, dates from Saxon times, but the oldest surviving part is the tower, constructed in 1130.

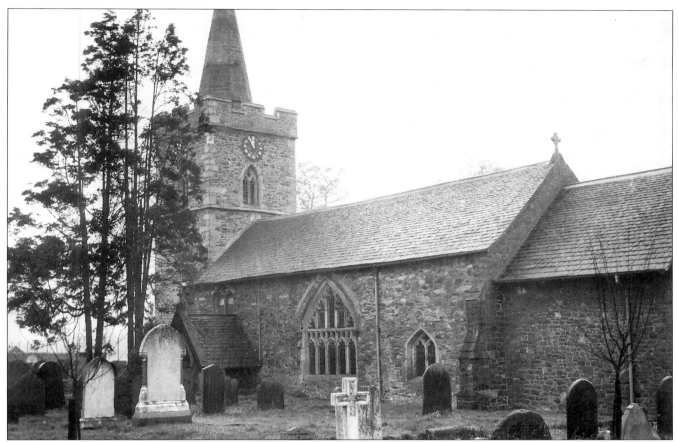

All Saints' Church, which stands in a beautiful setting near the little stream at the entrance to Bradgate Park.

Gracedieu Manor, the Catholic Preparatory School in the Charnwood Forest, in October 1953.

The St John the Baptist Church in King's Norton was erected at the expense of William Fortrey, who died in 1783.

A tranquil Langham around the turn of the century.

Long Whatton Village Church.

Members of the Peterborough Diocese Church Army pose for a photograph outside Belgrave Vicarage in the early years of this century.

Measham Methodists hold a garden party in 1902, in the garden of Mr Jordan, the local baker and grocer.

LEICESTERSHIRE AT WAR

After two years and seven months, the Boer War in South Africa is over in 1902. Leicester honours those who have fallen.

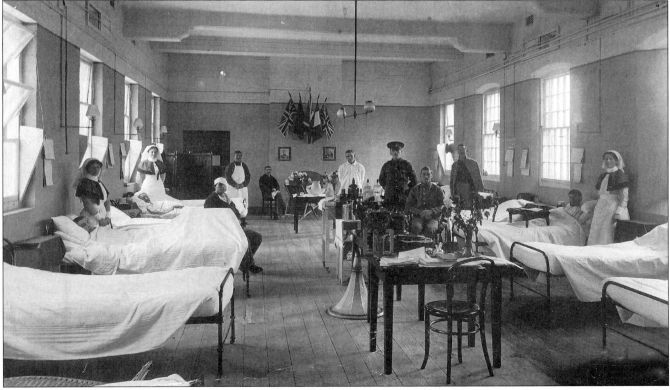

A ward for the wounded of World War One at the 5th Northern General Hospital, formerly The University Road, Leicester, Lunatic Asylum. It is now part of Leicester University. This picture was taken in 1915 or 1916.

During World War One, the Municipal Offices were used as a recruiting centre. The poster reads: '5,000 Leicester's now at the front. Ask 2,000 more Leicester men to join them.'

During World War One, a tram depot in Belgrave Gate became a main centre for shell production in Leicester.

Pictured outside Leicester Town Hall in January 1918, this British tank was used to drum up support for the war effort. On 20 November 1917, at Cambrai in France, tanks were used in warfare for the first time, causing havoc among the Germans.

Armistice Day, 11 November 1918, in Town Hall Square where the Lord Mayor of Leicester, Alderman Walter Lovell, announces the end of hostilities to a jubilant crowd.

The unveiling of the temporary War Memorial in Town Hall Square, Leicester, after World War One.

Oadby's War Memorial was dedicated in 1921.

Earl Haig
unveiled Ratby's
War Memorial
after World War
One.

The War Memorial on Victoria
Park, pictured in the 1920s with
a large group of children in
their Sunday best preparing for
a parade.

A blackout cover over a headlamp in January 1938, in preparation for wartime driving.

A happy party of London evacuees on their arrival at Wigston in October 1940.

A wartime photograph with the Clock Tower encased with hoardings asking Leicester folk for 7,660 volunteers to join the Air Raid Precautions in various posts.

Two women bus drivers of Midland Red in Leicester in December 1943. They are Miss Terry Dowd and Miss Margaret Ellison.

Two students at the Leicester College of Art & Technology learning the building trade with lessons in bricklaying in January 1942.

Girls learning a new occupation during World War Two, making camouflage nets at an RAOC depot in August 1941.

Land Army girls helping in the farm 'somewhere in Leicestershire' in September 1941.

Land Army girls giving a tasty snack to their favourite pony at the Leicester City Farms in February 1944.

A demonstration semi-mobile kitchen which visited Leicester with members of the Education staff, WVS and ETC preparing dinner in the open.

A large-scale civil and military exercise took place in Leicestershire in March 1943. Major Leggett (third from left) commanded one of the mobile defence forces and is seen here briefing his officers and NCOs.

Despatch riders assembled at a farmyard in Dunton Bassett during an exercise in March 1943. They were part of the invading force of 'enemy' troops.

How close the Luftwaffe came to interfering with the unbroken production of the *Leicester Mercury* in November 1940. The scene is Albion Street and a short distance away fire services and rescue workers fight a losing battle to save a shattered factory.

Bomb blast damage at the Town Hall in 1941. The blitz was recalled by Mrs Mary Owen. "I was terrified. I remember going to the top of Avebury Avenue and looking out over the town. I never saw anything like it. The whole town looked as though it was aflame."

American troops parade down Granby Street in 1944. The US 82nd Airborne were based in Leicestershire and parachuted into France on D-day during the Normandy invasion of June 1944.

VE Day celebrations in Town Hall Square in May 1945. World War Two is over and Leicester folk can look forward to the future after six long years of struggle.

Evacuees returning home in June 1945, at Leicester Railway Station

A memorial stained-glass window in Leicester Cathedral pays tribute to the local men who gave their lives for their country during World War Two.

LEISURE AND PLEASURE

Leicester Expo '72 took place in Abbey Park. The scheme was devised by a three-man design team at Leicester Polytechnic. It was a ten-day festival to make people take note of the city's achievements.

Seven young ladies picked to act as hostesses at Leicester's Expo '72. From the left are: Dorothy Shiel (23), of 41 Uppingham Road, Leicester; twins Avril and Gillian Lansdown (17), of 3 Beresford Drive, Leicester; Sheila Boughey (24), of 61 Snarestone Road, Newton Burgoland; Jane Mawbey (17), of 104 Glenhills Boulevard, Leicester; Mrs Lynne Hold (19), of 8 Georgeham Close, Wigston Magna; and Kathleen Marriott (22), of 134 New Walk, Leicester.

Attractive programme sellers wearing their Expo '72 outfits, mingling with the crowds at the City of Leicester Show at Abbey Park, are Mrs Lynne Hold, of Wigston Magna (trying on the bearskin) and Sheila Boughey from Newton Burgoland. The Guardsman is James Richardson, from Tamworth.

The famous figure of Daniel Lambert features more than once in the Expo story. Leicester's fat man (played by Frank Billings) appears in the Great Tent Show, and a special Daniel Lambert Wine was on offer to boost the conviviality of the occasion.

Tom Thumb, who stood only 29ins high, with his showman Mons Ugo. The American midget made an appearance at the New Hall (now the Belvoir Street Lending Library) in Leicester.

Winner and finalists of the Expo secretarial competition. Second left is the winner herself, Mrs Gillian Grenfell, 30 Belvoir Drive, Leicester, who was named 'Miss Secretary of Leicester'. With her are the other 'Miss Secretary' finalists. Mrs Mary Lancaster and Mrs Pauline Donnelly (right), and stage, screen and television actor Bill Maynard, who made the presentation. The title 'Miss Commercial Student of Leicester' went to Angela Hopkins, 31 Bradbourne Road.

Charles Bennion (1857-1929), who presented Bradgate Park to the people of Leicestershire in 1928, was managing director of the British United Shoe Machine Co. Ltd.

Leicester's first Lord Mayor, James Thomas, in 1928. During his year of office, he was renowned for his success in launching a campaign drawing the attention of the world to Leicester's products and advantages. He died in 1950.

PC John William Stephens, of the *Leicester Borough Police Force*, pictured directing traffic at the Clock Tower. 'Tubby' was England's heaviest constable, weighing in at 24st. He is thought to have inspired the evergreen hit song *The Laughing Policeman*. Leicester songwriter Lawrence Wright also dedicated *Pride of the Force* to him. PC Stephens died in 1908, aged 48.

Barlestone Band pictured at the turn of the century.

The days of pierrots and concert parties before radio and television. They show The Hamorils, one of The Superiors and one of The Black and White Pierrots with The Spagettis Maccaroni Rag Time Band.

Leon and his orchestra, who used to perform at Boot's Tea Rooms.

Prima ballerina Alicia Markova danced at the Little Theatre in Leicester on 31 May 1934, when she was only 24.

The great Russian-born ballerina, Anna Pavlova, pictured beside a train at Leicester's Central Railway Station. Six weeks later, in January 1931, she died of pleurisy at The Hague.

The 'Birstall Lighthouse' wooden tower, constructed in 1909 to transmit and receive wireless signals. It stood in the garden of 91 Park Road and was in use until 1913.

Local retailer Samuel May with the first television set in Leicester in 1936.

In 1959, a Murphy record player and VHF medium and long wave receiver sold for £57 15s 0d. A Murphy six-valve AC/DC table set for the reception of VHF sold for £20 9s 6d in 1959. The Ekcovision television set – a press-button receiver for the fast-growing 23ins market. It sold for 76 guineas in 1964.

Rock & Roll comes to Leicester in March 1957. The caption reads: 'Dig this! Clear the floor, the cats are in town!'

Two fire appliances outside Leicester's Palais de Danse on the morning of 27 September 1960 – and the posters advertise a 'Redecoration Ball' for the following week.

Hot Stuff from Leicester were the winners of Crocodillo/Radio Luxembourg Roadshow Supertroupers Disco Dance Team Championships held in November 1981. They won a Talbot Rancho. Pictured with them is D.J. Tony Prince.

A tranquil scene in the early part of this century in the back garden of Thomas and Ruth Palmer. The house is in Pool Road, off Fosse Road North.

A Harvest Festival display at St John's School, Clarendon Park, Leicester, in the 1920s.

Two youngsters seen enjoying the last days of their 1961 summer holidays fishing the canal at Foxton.

Leicester's Pearly King and Queen, Ernie and Betty White, with market traders in a knees-up at the start of the Leicester Market Centenary celebration in 1984.

Roger Chapman, lead singer with Family, the famous local band, belts out another number during a concert in the early 1970s. They made the Top 10 album charts on numerous occasions with their brand of Underground Music. Other members of the band were John Whitney, Ric Grech, Jim King, Rob Townsend, John Welder, John Palmer and Harry Overnall.

Englebert Humperdinck, the Leicester lad who became a worldwide celebrity, having Top 10 hit singles and albums. Previously, of course, he was known as Gerry Dorsey.

Showwaddywaddy, seen here performing at De Montfort Hall in November 1979, were perhaps Leicester's best known pop group.

A charity performance of Rip Van Winkle by the Leicester Amateur Music and Dramatic Society in 1913.

The Cameo Cinema, High Street, pictured in June 1971. The film then showing was *Hello Dolly*.

Leicester's Floral Hall on Belgrave Gate was converted from a skating rink in 1910. It was bought, along with the Palace Theatre, by Sketchley early in 1959 to house a modern cleaning plant. It had championed the cause of British films during the early 1920s.

The Co-operative Hall in Belgrave Gate in April 1960, considered by some to be the 'ugliest building' in Leicester.

The Lawn Cinema, Birstall, was demolished in February 1971 to make way for a supermarket.

Playwright Joe Orton was born in Leicester in 1933 and lived at 9 Fayhurst Road. He was educated at Marriott Road School. His first play, *Entertaining Mr Sloan* (1964), was voted Best Play of the Year. He went on to write *Loot* (1966) and *What The Butler Saw* (1967). Joe Orton met a tragic end, murdered by his lover, Kenneth Halliwell, in August 1967.

The Wigston Magna Cinema in August 1963. One of the films showing was *What ever happened to Baby Jane?*

'A little bit off the top' as the frontage of the Palace Theatre starts to disappear from Belgrave Gate in 1959.

The Prince and Princess of Wales, later King Edward VII and Queen Alexandra, at The Market Place on 29 May 1882.

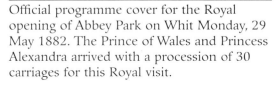

Official programme cover for the Royal opening of Abbey Park on Whit Monday, 29 May 1882. The Prince of Wales and Princess Alexandra arrived with a procession of 30 carriages for this Royal visit.

King Edward VII, with a fox terrier, waiting at Saxby Station in 1907.

King George VI and Queen Elizabeth visit Imperial Typewriters on 30 October 1946. Pictured with them is Mr Joseph Holland Goddard, Imperial's chairman, who was knighted three years later. The late Mr Goddard was also chairman of Wadkin Ltd and chairman of the National Steel Foundation Ltd of Fifeshire.

HRH Princess Alexandra opens the new *Leicester Mercury* building in 1967.

The Queen and the Duke of Edinburgh, visiting Leicester in May 1958, are met by the Lord Mayor, Alderman Frederick Jackson, and his wife.

The bust of Earl Beatty of Brooksby and the North Sea at the village church in Brooksby. The admiral, who commanded the British fleet at Heligoland in 1914 and at Jutland in 1916, died in 1936.

Family gathering during haymaking in the fields which once surrounded the Wyggeston Hospital at the corner of Fosse Road South and Hinckley Road. Mr Harry North, butcher for many years on Hinckley Road, rented these fields. This photograph was taken about 1910.

The Royal Daimler leaves a bedecked London Road Railway Station carrying the King and Queen on the 1946 Royal visit to Leicester.

The Holy Well in Ratby, which never runs dry or freezes, is said to have certain healing properties.

Leicester Town Waits, who used to herald the coming of Christmas. Up to the end of the 17th century, local authorities paid the 'Waits' to patrol the town.

The annual Humberstone Gate, Leicester fair. The last one was held in May 1904.

The annual Statutes Fair held in the Main Street of Ashby-de-la-Zouch. This one was in September 1955.

A troop of 'Cavaliers' pass under Rupert's Gateway and by the Old Castle Inn during the Pageant of Leicester in 1932.

A medieval procession moves past the main grandstand during the Pageant of Leicester in 1932.

A Coronation procession in June 1953 with girls in Elizabethan costumes leading the Shoe Princess's carriage which is pulled by Shetland ponies.

William Carey's Cottage, in Harvey Lane which, it was decided, should be preserved.

Interior view of William Carey's Cottage.

A tea party, to celebrate Lord Curzon's coming of age, in the riding school on the Gopsall estate in Norton in 1905.

One of the last cheese fairs to be held in Leicester was staged in the Market Place near the Duke of Rutland's statue near the Corn Exchange. There were two cheese fairs each year, in May and in October. The cheeses were mainly Red Leicestershire from the Ullesthorpe district, and Stilton from the Melton Mowbray area.

Nomination day in 1906 in Market Bosworth. The Conservative candidate, Mr Allen H.P. Stoneham, is seen surrounded by local townsfolk.

The kindergarten class at Belmont House School in 1878. The boy with the blond curly hair sitting on the knee of the lady with the white blouse is Percy Gee who was Pro-Chancellor of Leicester University. Belmont House is now the Belmont Hotel.

Boating on Humberstone Park, which ceased with the outbreak of war in 1939.

The King Richard III commemorative tablet in its new setting (above) and its previous position in the gable end of the building (right).

A peaceful afternoon's croquet in 1860 at the Old Rectory in Gaulby. The house was renamed Greyladies.

Thorncroft, once the residence of the Thomas Cook, is now the Leicestershire branch of the British Red Cross Society on London Road. Cook's first large-scale railway trip, to a Temperance rally at Loughborough, took place on 5 July 1841.

John Bunyan and John Wesley plaque on the Dryads building in St Nicholas Street in 1959.

Cardigan House, Burton Street, Melton Mowbray, was the hunting lodge of Lord Cardigan, who led the Light Brigade at Balaclava in 1854.

Elgin Lodge, off Scalford Road, Melton Mowbray, the former home of the famous painter John Ferneley.

The Abbey Park monument to Cardinal Thomas Wolsey, who died in 1530.

Queniborough Old Hall, with its many gables, unique and elegant arches and grey-green Groby slated roof, had not been much altered in January 1955 since Prince Rupert, commanding the Royalist forces, made his headquarters there in 1642 during the English Civil War. Highwayman Dick Turpin is said to have hidden there about the time of his legendary ride to York.

The Quorn Hunt on Belton village green in 1966.

The deputy treasurer to the City of Leicester, Mr J.B. Hughes, receives the traditional rent of a damask rose and four pennies from licensee Mr James Smith and his wife Joan in 1969. It was laid down in 1636 when shoemaker James Teele purchased the land for £2.

When Alderman Thomas Blunt, who died in January 1663, he bequeathed the sum of five shillings to be given to the Lord Mayor of Leicester every year, just before Christmas, to buy himself a pair of gloves. In 1971, Alderman Percy Watts was presented with a Churchill crown piece by Mr David Colver, senior administrative assistant.

'Great chiefton o' the puddin' race...' Leicester City manager Jock Wallace pierces the haggis at a Burns Night celebration organised by former City winger Charlie Adams. Others in the picture are Ken Chisholm (left), who was Adams' partner on the left wing in City's 1949 FA Cup Final team, and Notts County manager Jimmy Sirrel (second from left).

Annual sale of the wether at the Nag's Head in Enderby. The wether is a piece of land at Ratby which was given to the villagers by John of Gaunt in 1390 as a reward for entertaining him at the spring fair. Mr Bernard Woolman 'bought' the field for £7 in 1966. He is seated second from the right.

The Vicar of Sileby Parish Church, the Revd Raymond J. Hunting, presents oranges to the Rose Queen and children under a 600-year-old elm tree in May 1973. An old tradition, it was revived ten years earlier.

Molly dancers from the Hinckley Bullockers drink a toast to the plough outside the Lord Bassett Arms in Sapcote on Plough Monday in 1994, the first Monday after Twelfth Night.

Market Bosworth Young Farmers' Club keeping the tradition of blessing the plough alive in 1985.

The start of the gruelling Great Glen brook race in May 1980.

Youthful merrymakers around the Maypole at Bitteswell May Day celebrations in 1964.

Maypole dancing 65 years ago in Belton, near Loughborough. The pole is still there today.

Before the start of the Hallaton Bottle Kicking on Easter Monday 1937.

A celebration drink by a Medbourne supporter at the 1962 Hallaton Bottle Kicking.

Revd Thomas J. Preece, rector of Hallaton Church, helps cut the hare pie early this century. This was another tradition of the Hallaton Bottle Kicking.

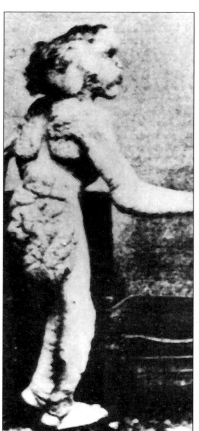

Joseph Merrick, 'The Elephant Man', was born in Leicester in 1862 and by the time he was five his forehead, right arm and feet were horribly deformed. At 17 he entered the Union Workhouse and during his stay Charles Marriott, senior surgeon at Leicester Infirmary, removed flesh resembling an elephant's trunk from his upper lip. At 24 Merrick put himself on exhibition in Leicester, Nottingham and London and two years later was touring in Europe. His last years were spent in a London hospital where he was visited by many famous people. Joseph Merrick died in 1890, shortly before his 28th birthday.

Lord Charles Percy Snow, or C.P. Snow (1905-1980), the physicist and novelist, author of the essay *The Two Cultures of the Scientific Revolution* and a sequence of novels *Strangers and Brothers* (11 volumes) and his most famous *Corridors of Power* in 1964, was born in Richmond Road, Aylestone. He was made a life peer in 1965.

Una Stubbs, star of *Till Death Us Do Part, Give us a Clue,* and Aunt Sally in *Worzel Gummidge*, lived in Burbage from the age of two until she was seven. Her father worked in a local hosiery factory.

Gertie Gitana: *There's an old mill by the stream, Nellie Dean, Where we used to sit and dream, Nellie Dean* was made famous by Getrude Ross who is buried in Wigston Cemetery. As Gertie Gitana she played music-halls across the country from 1907 to 1937. She married Wigston-born impressario Don Ross in 1928. Gertie died in London in 1937.

Sir Richard and Sir David Attenborough with the Lord Mayor of Leicester in 1990 after being made Freemen of the City. Their family moved to Leicester in 1932 when their father was appointed Principal of University College. Richard attended Wyggeston Grammar School and then went up to Clare College, Cambridge. After two years in the Royal Navy and a job in a publishing house, he joined the BBC in 1952 as a trainee producer. Between 1954 and 1975 he went on zoological expeditions across the world. He has appeared on television in numerous wildlife programmes from 1976 to 1993 including *Wildlife on One*, *Life on Earth*, *The Living Plane*t and *Trials of Life*. His 12 books started with *Zoo Quest to Guinea* in 1956 to *Life on Earth* in 1979. He has 21 honorary doctorates, was made a knight in 1985. Born in 1923, three years before his brother, Sir Richard Attenborough attended the same school as his brother before going to the Royal Academy of Dramatic Art. His London stage career lasted from 1941 to 1958 but as a film star, director and producer he is best known with over 50 films to his credit including *In Which We Serve, Brighton Rock, I'm Alright Jack, The Great Escape, Dr Dolittle, 10 Rillington Place* and *Jurassic Park*. In the early 1960s he produced *Whistle Down The Wind* and the *L-Shaped Room*, then went on to direct four films in the 1970s including *Young Winston* and *A Bridge Too Far*. He has also produced and directed five films, *Oh What A Lovely War*, which won 16 international awards, and *Gandhi*, which gained 19 accolades. He was knighted in 1976.

Sir Malcolm Sargent was organist and choirmaster at St Mary's, Melton Mowbray, from 1914 to 1924. He was only 19 when he received a Bachelor of Music degree. By the age of 24 he was a Doctor of Music. Sir Malcolm is widely acknowledged as one of the greatest English conductors. He died in 1967 and St Mary's has a special memorial window in the chancel to commemorate his life.

SPORTING HEROES

Leicester Fosse players in 1901-02. (The name change came in July 1919.) Fosse finished 14th in Division Two and lost 1-0 to Glossop in the FA Cup this season.

Leicester City Football Club in 1921-22. Note the press boxes in the background.

Leicester City FC, 1924-25 season, when they won the Second Division championship but lost 2-1 to Cardiff City in the fourth round of the FA Cup.

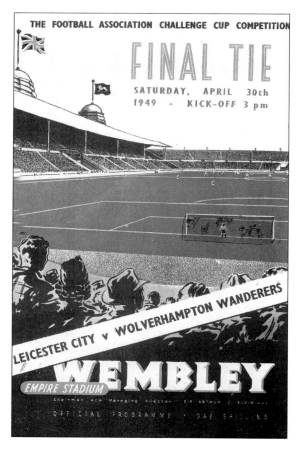

Leicester City played in four FA Cup Finals between 1949 and 1969, unfortunately losing them all. This is the cover of the programme for the 1949 game at Wembley, when they lost to Wolverhampton Wanderers.

The Duke of Edinburgh shakes hands with Leicester City manager John Duncan before the 1949 FA Cup Final against Wolves at Wembley.

The Wolves goalkeeper Bert Williams collects the ball from a Leicester City forward during the 1949 FA Cup Final.

Norman Plummer, the City captain, and Billy Wright, skipper of Wolves, shake hands before the 1949 Cup Final which City lost 3-1.

City's 1949 Cup Final team parades through the streets of Leicester to be greeted by well wishers.

Leicester City's team for the 1961 FA Cup Final against Tottenham Hotspur at Wembley. Back Row (left to right): Colin Appleton, Ian King, Len Chalmers, Gordon Banks, Frank McLintock, Richie Norman. Front Row: Howard Riley, Jimmy Walsh, Hughie Mclimoyle, Ken Keyworth and Albert Cheesebrough.

Jimmy Walsh, Dave Mackay (centre) and Spurs goalkeeper Bill Brown in an incident at the 1961 Cup Final.

Crowds line London Road to welcome back the losing Cup Finalists in 1961 after City had gone down 2-0 to Tottenham.

The cover of the 1963 FA Cup Final programme when Leicester City met Manchester United.

The Duke of Edinburgh is introduced to Leicester players before the 1963 FA Cup Final. From the left are Colin Appleton, Ken Keyworth, Mike Stringfellow and Richie Norman.

Gordon Banks climbs high to deny Manchester United's Noel Cantwell at Wembley in May 1963.

A sad moment for City as skipper Colin Appleton receives an FA Cup runners-up medal from the Queen. It was second time in three years that Leicester had fallen at the final hurdle.

Leicester City aboard a Midland Red coach at the Town Hall Square in May 1963. They had just lost another FA Cup Final, this time 3-1 to Manchester United.

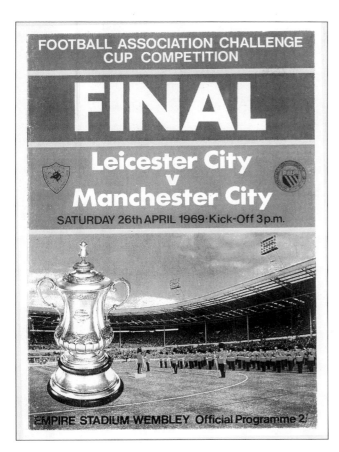

The cover of the
1969 FA Cup
Final programme.

Princess Anne meets the
Leicester team before the 1969
FA Cup Final against
Manchester City.

Leicester City's Peter Shilton dives at the feet of Francis Lee and Neil Young of Manchester City while City's Graham Cross runs in. Leicester lost 1-0 to a goal from Young in the 1969 FA Cup Final at Wembley.

City start their procession through the streets of Leicester from London Road Station to the Town Hall following their defeat in the 1969 FA Cup Final.

Leicester City goalkeeper Gordon Banks. Banks and another Leicester goalkeeper, Peter Shilton, were probably the most outstanding 'keepers in English international football's history. Banks won 73 caps for his country and made 356 appearances for City. He gained a World Cup winners' medal with England in 1966 before losing the sight of an eye in a road accident.

March 1985 and Gary Lineker (right), one of Leicester City's most famous players, accepts the congratulations of teammates after yet another goal. He had just been named for a second England cap.

Peter Shilton runs out for Stoke City against Leicester in a League match at Filbert Street in January 1975 following his transfer to the Potters in November 1974.

Peter Shilton signs full-time professional forms for Leicester City as a 17-year-old under the gaze of Matt Gillies, City's manager at that time. Shilton's goalkeeping exploits are legendary. He achieved 1,000 senior appearances – including 339 for Leicester – and won 125 England caps. He also played for Stoke City, Nottingham Forest, Southampton and Derby County at the highest level. Born in Leicester on 18 September 1949, Shilton became City's youngest-ever First Division debutant at 16, keeping a clean sheet in his first game when he was still an apprentice. He was awarded the MBE in 1986 and the OBE in 1991.

This Fleckney Guild team won the Market Harborough KO Cup in 1926.

The East Langton Ladies cricket team pictured around 1902. They played many matches each summer, including some games against men's teams.

Wheelbarrow racing was a popular form of physical challenge at athletic sports meetings 100 years ago. This was the start of the final of a quarter-mile event on the old Belgrave Road Ground in May 1895, held in aid of the Institution for the Blind.

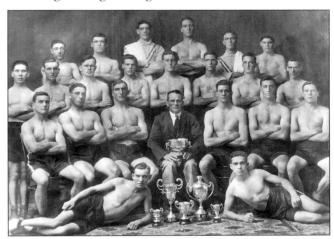

The Leicestershire Regiment's 2nd Battalion boxing team pictured in the early 1920s when they were serving in India.

Johnny Williams, Old Millhillians' international scrum-half, throws out a long one before Gordon Almey, Leicester Tigers' wing forward, can get at him in December 1959, in the annual Christmas match against the Barbarians. Tigers lost 17-9.

A day at the races. The finishing post at Leicester Racecourse in the early 1950s.

A view from mid-wicket for members at the 'Meet' at Grace Road, in August 1967. Leicestershire moved back there after earlier playing at Aylestone Road.

Leicestershire skipper Ray Illingworth holds the John Player Sunday League trophy won by the county in 1977. A former Yorkshire and England captain, Illingworth became a controversial chairman of the England selectors in the 1990s.

The Hollywood Motor Rodeo team gave a show at Leicester stadium in May 1955.

This is the 1960 Monte Carlo Rally team from Leicester and county with their Vauxhall Cresta. Left to right are Frank Dimblebee, John Walker and John Sturgess. They were pilot, rally and racing driver and stock car driver respectively.

Leicester Lions speedway team at Blackbird Road in April 1968. Back Row (left to right): Norman Storer, John Hart, Ron Wilson (team manager), John Boulger, Vic White. Front: Anders Michanek, Ray Wilson (seated on bike, the captain), and George Major.

The winner! Leicester boxer Jack Gardner is seen here after winning the British heavyweight championship in July 1950 by beating Johnny Williams, who has collapsed in his corner. Gardner later won the European heavyweight crown in March 1951, beating Joe Weidin.

Leicester snooker star Willie Thorne wins the Mercantile Credit Classic in 1985.

SUBSCRIBERS

Mr R J Adams
John Atkinson
Sue & Alan Bannister
Mr & Mrs Eric Bown
Jose & Terry Brown
Steven Brown, Wigston
Mr T Brakes
Gina Brooks
Mrs S E Busby
Mrs M Bruce
Anne & David Carpenter
David Carrington
Alan Carter
B Chaplin
William G Checkland
Sylvia Cieslak
T Coates
Bryan Cooper
A V Curtis
Mrs P V Corkill
Marjorie Deane
Barry H Derbyshire
Keith Dickens
J Dowell
John & Di Driver
Mrs Rose Eagle
Marjorie & John Farmer
Anne Fitzgerald
Cyril T Flynn, Des Moines, USA
Mr & Mrs B Fox, Port Elizabeth, South Africa
Mr Roy Hunt, New Zealand
David Gillard
Richard Graves
Kay Gowland
Mrs Maud Greet
Nicholas & Shirley Hales
John Hardy
Anne & Paul Harris
Mr T H Harris
Peter Hooke
Josephine Humberston
Mr J G Illston
Chris Jinks
Adam Jones
Ann & Colin Jordan

T F J Johnson
Andrew W King & Mark E Balding
Robert A Leake
Mr Colin Lindley
William, Sam and George Loveday
K F Marvin
Jan & Bill Murden
Marian & Roy Measures
Ron Measures
Professor David Barry Mobbs
Mrs B M I Nocton
Adrian Norton
Mr Trevor Overton, BEM
Norman Pilgrim
Sharynn Porch
Barbara Kennedy Plumb
Neville Pratt, Melbourne, Australia
Richard Pratt, Johnsonville, Australia
Gillian Prince
David Rhodes
Mr R Roberts
Harvey Robinson
Anthony Roe
Henrietta Schultka
A J Sherriff
Miss M R Stacey
Aubrey & Judith Stevenson
Bernard Smith
Neville & May Smith
N G Smith
Mr Patrick Smith
Peter & Judy Smith
D C & M A Tasker
Jessie Taylor
Richard Taylor
Michael Thompson
Beryl & Ernie Timmis
Mr & Mrs D Turpin
E W Varnam
Mr Eric W Varnam
John Ward
Roger Ernest Ward
Eileen Wilcox
Mrs M S Wright